Dealing with Worry...

Worried

T0080605

Isabel Thomas

Illustrated by Clare Elsom

Heinemann
LIBRARY
Chicago, Illinois

© 2013 Heinemann Library
an imprint of Capstone Global Library, LLC
Chicago, Illinois

All rights reserved. No part of this publication may be reproduced or transmitted in any form or by any means, electronic or mechanical, including photocopying, recording, taping, or any information storage and retrieval system, without permission in writing from the publisher.

Edited by Dan Nunn, Rebecca Rissman, and Catherine Veitch
Designed by Philippa Jenkins
Original illustrations © Clare Elsom
Illustrated by Clare Elsom
Production by Victoria Fitzgerald
Originated by Capstone Global Library, Ltd.

Library of Congress Cataloging-in-Publication Data
Thomas, Isabel, 1980-
Worried / Isabel Thomas.
p. cm.—(Dealing with feeling)
Includes bibliographical references and index.
ISBN 978-1-4329-7110-6 (hb)—ISBN 978-1-4329-7119-9 (pb) 1. Worry in children—Juvenile literature. 2. Worry—Juvenile literature. I. Title.
BF723.W67T56 2013
152.4'6—dc23 2012008397

Every effort has been made to contact copyright holders of material reproduced in this book. Any omissions will be rectified in subsequent printings if notice is given to the publisher.

All the Internet addresses (URLs) given in this book were valid at the time of going to press. However, due to the dynamic nature of the Internet, some addresses may have changed, or sites may have changed or ceased to exist since publication. While the author and publisher regret any inconvenience this may cause readers, no responsibility for any such changes can be accepted by either the author or the publisher.

Printed in the United States 5920

Contents

What Is Worry? 4
What Does It Feel Like to Be Worried? 6
How Do We Know When Someone Is Worried? .. 8
Is It Normal to Feel Worried? 10
How Can I Deal with Worries? 12
Why Is It Good to Share My Worries? 14
What If I Can't Talk About My Feelings? 16
Why Should I Deal with Worries? 18
How Can I Help Someone Who Is Feeling Worried? 20
Make a Worry Toolbox 22
Glossary 23
Find Out More 24
Index 24

Some words are shown in bold, **like this**. Find out what they mean in the glossary on page 23.

What Is Worry?

Worry is a **feeling**. It is normal to have many kinds of feelings every day.

Some feelings are not nice to have. Worry is not a nice feeling. We feel worried when we think something bad might happen.

What Does It Feel Like to Be Worried?

Sometimes we might feel worried for a short time. When you are **nervous**, it can feel like there are butterflies in your stomach.

Sometimes worries can be very strong and last for a long time. It can be difficult to stop thinking about them.

How Do We Know When Someone Is Worried?

Our faces and bodies can show other people how we are feeling. **Feelings** can change the way that people behave, too.

Some people get grumpy when they are worried, even with their friends. Other people try to hide their worries. This can make them feel worse.

Is It Normal to Feel Worried?

Some changes are exciting. Others can make you feel worried. It is normal to feel worried about a big change, such as moving to a new house or school.

Take breaks from worrying by doing something you enjoy. There are other things you can do to help yourself feel better, too.

How Can I Deal with Worries?

Sometimes things you see on the Internet or television can make you feel scared. It can be hard to deal with worries on your own.

Ask a grown-up to **explain** what you have seen. Finding out more about something can make it feel less scary.

Why Is It Good to Share My Worries?

When somebody in your family gets sick, it can make you feel very worried. Talking about your worries can make you feel better.

A grown-up can help you understand what is going on. Sometimes the thoughts inside our heads are very different from what is really happening.

What If I Can't Talk About My Feelings?

Imagine you are worried because somebody is **bullying** you or your friend. You might be scared that telling a grown-up will make it worse.

Other times, it is hard to put **feelings** into words. Try drawing a picture of your worries instead, and show it to a grown-up whom you trust.

Why Should I Deal with Worries?

Keeping worries inside can make you feel worse. Worries can get in the way and stop you from enjoying fun things.

You might not be able to **concentrate** in school. The best way to deal with **feelings** is to talk about them.

How Can I Help Someone Who Is Feeling Worried?

Everyone feels worried sometimes, even grown-ups. When people you know are worried, they might want to talk about how they feel.

You can help by listening. Sometimes, just sharing worries with someone makes the worries go away.

Make a Worry Toolbox

Write down some tips to help you deal with worried **feelings.**

Glossary

bullying when a person harms or is nasty to somebody

concentrate focus all your attention on something, so that you can do it well

explain describe something in a way that makes it easier to understand

feeling something that happens inside our minds. It can affect our bodies and the way we behave.

nervous scared or worried about doing something

Find Out More

Books

Henkes, Kevin. *Wemberly Worried.* New York: Greenwillow, 2010.

Medina, Sarah. *Worried* (Feelings). Chicago: Heinemann Library, 2007.

Wolff, Ferida. *Is a Worry Worrying You?* Terre Haute, Ind.: Tanglewood, 2007.

Internet sites

Facthound offers a safe, fun way to find Internet sites related to this book. All of the sites on Facthound have been researched by our staff.

Here's all you do:
Visit www.facthound.com
Type in this code: 9781432971106

Index

big changes 10
feeling grumpy 9
feeling nervous 6
feeling scared 12, 13, 16
hiding worries 9, 18
listening 21
sharing worries 13, 21
talking 14, 16, 19, 20